THE MORE DESERVING CASES

Portrait of Robert Graves by H. A. Freeth, A.R.A.

THE MORE
DESERVING CASES

Eighteen Old Poems

for

Reconsideration

by

ROBERT GRAVES

Marlborough College Press

1962

FOREWORD

I AM SOMETIMES asked to reconsider long-discarded poems, and have kept a mental list of these, from which I recently picked out the more deserving cases. Many of them needed drastic abridgement as well as general amendment; others had been let go for personal reasons that no longer seemed cogent.

Eighteen of them are here resurrected, for however brief a new life, by the kindness of my great-nephew Martin Freeth, Master of the Chapel at Marlborough College, and his fellow-printers.

DEYA,
MAJORCA.   R.G.

CONTENTS

SULLEN MOODS

L OVE, do not count your labour lost
    Though I turn sullen or retired
    Even at your side; my thought is crossed
With fancies by no evil fired.

And when I answer you, some days,
    Vaguely and wildly, do not fear
That my love walks forbidden ways,
    Breaking the ties that hold it here.

If I speak gruffly, this mood is
    Mere indignation at my own
Shortcomings, plagues, uncertainties:
    I forget the gentler tone.

You, now that you have come to be
    My one beginning, prime and end,
I count at last as wholly me,
    Lover not longer nor yet friend.

Help me to see you as before
    When overwhelmed and dead, almost,
I stumbled on that secret door
    Which saves the live man from the ghost.

Be once again the distant light,
    Promise of glory, not yet known
In full perfection—wasted quite
    When on my imperfection thrown.

THE DIALECTICIANS

I HEARD two poets
    Down by the sea,
    Discussing a burdensome
Relativity.

Thought has a bias,
    Direction a bend,
Space its inhibitions,
    Time a dead end.

Is whiteness white?
    O then, call it black:
Farthest from the truth
    Is yet half-way back.

Effect ordains cause,
    Head swallowing the tail;
Does whale engulf sprat,
    Or sprat assume whale?

Contentions weary,
    It giddies to think;
Then swim, poet, swim!
    Or drink, poet, drink!

A VILLAGE FEUD

THE COTTAGE DAMSON, laden as could be,
Scowls at the Manor House magnolia-tree
That year by year within its thoughtless powers
Yields flowers and leaves and flowers and leaves and flowers,
While the Magnolia shudders as in fear:
'*Figurez-vous!* two sackfuls every year!'

4

THE CLIPPED STATER

(To Aircraftman 338171, *T. E. Shaw)*

KING ALEXANDER had been deified
By loud applause of the Macedonian phalanx,
By sullen groans of the wide worlds lately conquered.
Who but a god could have so engulphed their pride?

He did not take a goddess to his throne
In the elder style, remembering what disasters
Juno's invidious eye brought on her Consort.
Thais was fair; but he must hold his own.

Nor would he rank himself a common god
In fellowship with those of Ind or Egypt
Whom he had shamed; even to Jove his father
Paid scant respect (as Jove stole Saturn's nod).

Now meditates: 'No land of all known lands
Has offered me resistance, none denied me
Infinite power, infinite thought and knowledge;
What yet awaits the assurance of my hands?'

Alexander, in a fever of mind,
Reasons: 'Omnipotence by its very nature
Is infinite possibility and purpose,
Which must embrace *that it can be confined*.

'Then finity is true godhead's final test,
Nor does it dim the glory of free being.
I must fulfil myself by self-destruction.'
The curious phrase renews his conquering zest.

He assumes man's flesh. Djinn catch him up and fly
To a land of yellow folk beyond his knowledge,
And that he does not know them, he takes gladly
For surest proof he has put his godhead by.

In Macedonia shortly it is said:
'Alexander, our god, has died of a fever;
Demi-gods parcel out his huge dominions.'
So Alexander, as god, is duly dead.

But Alexander the man, whom yellow folk
Find roving naked, armed with a naked cutlass,
Has death, which is the stranger's fate, excused him.
Joyfully he submits to the alien yoke.

He is enrolled now in the frontier-guard
With gaol-birds and the press-gang's easy captures;
Where captains who have felt the Crown's displeasure,
But have thought suicide too direct and hard,

Teach him a new tongue and the soldier's trade,
To which the trade *he* taught has little likeness.
He glories in his foolish limitations:
At every turn his hands and feet are stayed.

'Who was your father, friend?' He answers: 'Jove.'
'His father?' 'Saturn.' 'And *his* father?' 'Chaos.'
'And *his*?' Thus Alexander loses honour:
Ten fathers is the least that a man should prove.

Stripes and bastinadoes, famine and thirst—
All these he suffers, never in resolution
Shaken, nor in his heart inquiring whether
Gods by their fiats can be self-accursed.

Thus he grows grey and eats his frugal rice,
Endures his watch on the fort's icy ramparts,
Staring across the uncouth leagues of desert,
Furbishes leather and steel; or shakes the dice.

He will not dream Olympianly, nor stir
To enlarge himself with comforts or promotion,
Nor yet evade the rack when, sour of temper,
He has tweaked a corporal's nose and called him 'cur'.

His comrades mutinously demand their pay—
'We have had none since the Emperor's Coronation.
At one gold piece a year there are fifteen owing.
One-third that sum would buy us free,' they say.

The pay-sack came at length, when hope was cold,
Though much reduced in bulk since its first issue
By the Chief Treasurer; and he, be certain,
Kept back one third of the silver and all the gold.

Every official hand had dipped in the sack;
And the frontier captains, themselves disappointed
Of long arrears, took every doit remaining;
But from politeness put a trifle back.

They informed the men: 'since no pay has come through,
We will advance from our too lavish purses
To every man of the guard, a piece of silver.
Let it be repaid when you get your overdue.'

The soldiers, grumbling but much gratified
By hopes of a drink and a drab, accept the favour;
And Alexander, advancing to the pay-desk,
Salutes and takes his pittance without pride.

The coin is bored, to string with the country's bronze
On a cord, and one side scraped to glassy smoothness;
But the head, clipped of its hair and neck, bears witness
That it had a broad, more generous mintage once.

Alexander, gazing at it then,
Greets it as an Alexandrian stater
Coined from the bullion taken at Arbela.
How came it here among these slant-eyed men?

He stands in a troubled reverie of doubt
Till a whip stings his shoulders and a voice bellows:
'Are you dissatisfied, you spawn of the ditches?'
So he salutes again and turns about,

More than uncertain what the event can mean.
Was his lost Empire, then, not all-embracing?
And how can the stater, though defaced, owe service
To a power that is as if it had never been?

'Must I renew my godhead?' But well he knows
Nothing can change the finite course resolved on;
He spends the coin on a feast of fish and almonds
And back to the ramparts briskly enough he goes.

EPITAPH ON AN UNFORTUNATE ARTIST

H E FOUND a formula for drawing comic rabbits :
    This formula for drawing comic rabbits paid,
    So in the end he could not change the tragic habits
This formula for drawing comic rabbits made.

THE CORNER KNOT

I WAS A CHILD and overwhelmed : Mozart
Had snatched me up fainting and wild at heart
To a green land of wonder, where estranged
I dipped my feet in shallow brooks, I ranged
Rough mountains, and fields yellow with small vetch :
Of which, though long I tried, I could not fetch
One single flower away, nor from the ground
Pocket one pebble of the scores I found
Twinkling enchanted there. So for relief
'I'll corner-knot,' said I, 'this handkerchief,
Faithful familiar that, look, here I shake
In these cool airs for proof that I'm awake.'
I tied the knot, the aspens all around
Heaved, and the river-banks were filled with sound ;
Which failing presently, the insistent loud
Clapping of hands returned me to the crowd.
I felt and, fumbling, took away with me
The knotted witness of my ecstasy,
Though flowers and streams were vanished past recall,
The aspens, the bright pebbled reach and all.

But now, grown older, I suspect Mozart
Himself had been snatched up by curious art
To my green land : estranged and wild at heart
He too had crossed the brooks, essayed to pick
That yellow vetch with which the plains are thick ;
And being put to it (as I had been)
To smuggle back some witness of the scene,
Had knotted up his cambric handkerchief
With common music, rippling, flat and brief ;
And home again, had sighed above the score
'Ay, a remembrancer, but nothing more.'

DEATH OF THE FARMER

'WHAT ails the Master, do I think?
Undoubtedly,' the Ox cried, 'drink,
That stupifies the spirit, dims
The reason, dulls the limbs.'

'He's done no good about the farm
These fifteen years, but only harm.
As well you know,' the old Ass said,
'We often wish him dead.'

'How hopefully at his Son's birth
We preached the reign of Heaven on Earth.
And sang him praises high and low.
Ay, that was long ago!'

'Still, to ensure domestic peace,
We tell the turkeys, ducks and geese:
"He rules, omniscient and great,
Proof-armoured against fate."

' "Granted," we say, "he's no more seen
Tending fat sheep in pastures green,
Or scattering at the break of morn
Largesse, profuse, of corn.

' "Yet, from some glorious inner room,
He guides the cowman, steward or groom,
And posts his ledger, page by page,
In joy or solemn rage.

' "Our feeding and our water-time,
Our breeding and our slaughter-time,
The dyke, the hedge, the plough, the cart—
These thoughts lie next his heart."

'The simple birds believe it true,
What now, poor poultry, will they do,
Dazed to confusion, when the glum
Gloved undertakers come,

'Tilting the coffin past the pond,
The ricks, the clamps, the yard beyond,
Skirting the midden-heap with care,
Then out, we know not where?'

VIRGIL THE SORCERER

V IRGIL, as the old Germans have related,
      Meaning a master-poet of wide fame—
      And yet their Virgil stands dissociated
From the suave hexametrist of that name,

Maro, whose golden and lick-spittle tongue
   Served Caesar's most un-Roman tyrannies,
Whose easy-flowing Georgics are yet sung
   As declamations in the academies—

Not Mantuan Virgil but another greater
   Who at Toledo first enlarged his spells,
Virgil, sorcerer, prestidigitator,
   Armed with all power that flatters or compels.

He, says the allegory, once was thrown
   By envious dukes into a dungeon keep
Where, vermin-scarred and wasting to the bone,
   Men crouched in year-old filth and could not sleep.

He beckoned then his bond-mates to his side,
   Commanding charcoal ; from a rusty grate
Charcoal they fetched him. Once again he cried
   'Where are the lordly souls, unbowed by fate,

'Eager to launch with me on midnight air
   A ship of hope, through the cold clouds to skim ?'
They gazed at Virgil in a quick despair
   Thinking him mad ; yet gently humoured him,

And watched his hand where on the prison wall
   He scratched a galley, buoyant and well-found.
'Bring sticks for oars!' They brought them at his call.
   'Up then and row!' They stepped from solid ground,

Climbed into fantasy and with a cheer
   Heaved anchor, bent their oars, pulled without stop.
Virgil was captain, Virgil took the steer
   And beached them, presently, on a mountain-top.

Here, without disillusion, all were free :
   Wrenching their fetters off, they went their ways.
A feat, they swore, that though it could not be,
   Was, in effect, accomplished beyond praise.

'Did Virgil do what legend has related?
   Is poetry in truth the queen of arts?
Can we hope better than a glib, bald-pated
   Self-laurelled Maro of agreeable parts?

Ah, fellow-captives, must you still condone
   The stench of evil? On a mound of mud
You loll red-eyed and wan, whittling a bone,
   Vermined, the low gaol-fever in your blood.

PYGMALION TO GALATEA

As YOU ARE WOMAN, so be lovely :
Fine hair afloat and eyes irradiate,
Long crafty fingers, fearless carriage,
And body lissom, neither short nor tall ;
So be lovely !

As you are lovely, so be merciful :
Yet must your mercy abstain from pity :
Prize your self-honour, leaving me with mine.
Love if you will ; or stay stone-frozen.
So be merciful !

As you are merciful, so be constant :
I ask not you should mask your comeliness,
Yet keep our love aloof and strange,
Keep it from gluttonous eyes, from stairway gossip.
So be constant !

As you are constant, so be various :
Love comes to sloth without variety.
Within the limits of our fair-paved garden
Let fancy like a Proteus range and change.
So be various !

As you are various, so be woman :
Graceful in going as well armed in doing.
Be witty, kind, enduring, unsubjected :
Without you I keep heavy house.
So be woman !

As you are woman, so be lovely :
As you are lovely, so be various,
Merciful as constant, constant as various.
So be mine, as I yours for ever.

DIPLOMATIC RELATIONS

KING GEORGE, still powder-grimed from Dettingen,
Called in thick tones : 'My Lord, fetch ink and pen.
I'll write a threatening note in my own hand.
This Chinese potentate must understand
That Britons have a boundless fame to brag.
No insult shall defile our glorious flag.
Two Bristol ships at Hankow fetching tea,
Boarded and robbed, at wharfside as they lay,
Of a costly cargo? Ha, Sir! Let me boast
My fleet stands ready to bombard your coast.
If meek apologies be not forthcoming
My fusiliers must through Pekin go drumming.
You shall eat dirt, d'ye hear, you knavish fellow,
Or we must tan your hide a deeper yellow.
Ten ships shall yearly visit your chief ports
With mirrors, beads, and clothing of all sorts,
Carrying decorum to your savage parts
With civilization, learning and the arts.
But if so much as a rattle's robbed or broke
Your Chinese territory flies up in smoke.
You then, beware! Signed, GEORGIUS REX. So, so.
Our Foreign Minister sends this. Take it, go!'

The Foreign Minister, reading the piece through,
Swore by his wig, why, this would never do.
'Our Sovereign trips on all the finer points
Of English speech, confuses, blurs, disjoints.
To send this note, 's blood, it were most unwise.
Suppose it intercepted by French spies?
'*La langue du roi...*' (I hear their mocking tome)
'Dunce-cap instead of crown, dunce-stool for throne !'
Why, even in China, men would laugh to read

This halting, odd, mis-spelt, improbable screed.
But stay! Our Sovereign we would surely please,
Translating him his Note into Chinese.
Li-Chung will do't, then there can be no call
To pawn our honour with the original. '

Li-Chung, the Bond Street tea-man with meek eyes
Performed the service, showing no surprise,
Though inwardly enraged and jealous for
The sacred majesty of his Emperor. . .
How faithful his translation, who can say?
George signed it readily, and it reached Cathay.

The Emperor from his Summer terraces
Claps hands for ink and sable paint-brushes
And writes with care a special declaration
To the Loyal Governor of the British Nation,
Commiserating with that luckless one
By seas exiled from his Imperial Sun
On such outcast and pariah-like condition:
'We note the abject tone of your petition
And sorry excuses for your impudence
In thus soliciting our Magnificence,
Then, though we cannot in the atlas hit on
A Chinese province (or sub-province) *Britain*,
We graciously will none the less allow
Ten yearly junks to harbour at Hankow
With skins, blubber, oil or such-like pelting stuff—
Indeed five junk-loads would be quite enough.
Formal permission signed, YOUR GOD. So, so.
Our Foreign Minister sends this. Take it! Go!'

The Foreign Minister, reading the piece through,
Swore by his pigtail, this would never do.
'Our Emperor neglects the niceties,

Indeed the major rules, of Court Chinese.
Our iron-helmed Manchu God in battle's shock
Or warrior council sits as firm as a rock,
But as for drafting edict, Note or letter. . .
My six-year-old could do as well, aye, better.
Can I permit my Sovereign's reputation
To sink even in a heathen's estimation?
I'll tactfully propose it more correct
To send this note in British dialect.
Ned Gunn the boxing-teacher at Nanking
Will soon translate the odd fantastic thing.'

Ned Gunn, a stolid sailor with bold eyes,
Performed the service, showing no surprise
Though, loyal to the death, he felt his gorge
Mount at this insult to victorious George.
His English version (which he owned was free)
The Emperor signed, frowned, sent oversea.

George read the note, puffed out his cheeks, began :
'He takes his medicine like a sensible man,
Apologizes humbly, swears to behave
With fawning loyalty of dog or slave,
Sadly admits his colour far from white
And trusts this missive is not impolite,
Longs for our British cargoes rich and strange,
Has only trash to offer in exchange.'
"May your Red, White and Blue still rule the main
And countless Dettingens be fought again!
God Save the King! Kow Tow! Success to barter." '
George swore : 'We must reward him with the Garter.'

THE PHILATELIST-ROYAL

THE Philatelist-royal
Was always too loyal
To say what he honestly
Thought of Philately.

Must it rank as a Science?
Then he had more reliance,
(As he told the Press wittily)
In Royal Philately
Than in all your geologies,
All your psychologies,
Bacteriologies,
Physics and such.
It was honester, much,
Free of mere speculations
And doubtful equations,
So therefore more true
From a pure science view
Than other school courses :
For Nature's blind forces
Here alone, they must own,
Played no meddlesome part.
It was better than Art :
It enforced education,
It strengthened the nation
In the arts of mensuration
And colour-discrimination,
In cleanliness, in hope,
In use of the microscope,
In mercantile transactions,
In a love of abstractions,
In geography and history :

It was a noble mystery.
So he told them again
That Philately's reign,
So mild and humane,
Would surely last longer,
Would surely prove stronger
Than the glory of Greece,
Than the grandeur of Rome.
It brought goodwill and peace
Wherever it found a home.
It was more democratic
More full, more ecstatic,
Than the Bible, the bottle,
The Complete Works of Aristotle,
And worthierer and betterer
And etceterier and etcetera.

The Philatelist-Royal
Was always too loyal
To say what he honestly
Thought of Philately.

TO BE LESS PHILOSOPHICAL

LISTEN, you theologians,
   Give ear, you rhetoricians,
   Hearken you, Aristotelians :
Of the Nature of God my song shall be.

Our God is infinite,
Your God is infinite,
Their God is infinite,
Of infinite generality.

God *he* is also finite,
God *she* is also definite,
He, she ; we, they ; you, each and it—
And likes to be correctly.

He is a bloody smart sergeant
And served in the Royal Artillery :
For gallantly exposing his person
He won the Victoria Cross.

She is also divorced
To a Russian count in exile
And paints a little and sings a little—
And won the Victoria Cross.

It has also the character of a soap
And may be used very freely
For disinfecting cattle trucks
And the very kine in the byre.

You are also mad, quite mad,
To imagine you are not God.
Goddam it, aren't you a Spirit,
And your ministers a flaming fire?

We are also gradually coming
To be less philosophical,
To speculate more confusedly
And defy the universal.

They are a very smart Victoria Cross
With the character of a soap a little :
They disinfect confusedly
To be less philosophical.

Each is a very smart Russian count
And may each be served very freely,
Freely, freely in the Royal Artillery
To be each less philosophical.

VARIABLES OF GREEN

GRASS-GREEN and aspen-green,
Laurel-green and sea-green,
Fine-emerald-green,
And many another hue :
As green commands the variables of green
So love my many loves of you.

DEVILISHLY PROVOKED

DEVILISHLY provoked
 By my officious pen—
 Where I demand one word
It scrawls me nine or ten ;
But each surviving word
 Resentfully I make
Sweat for those nine or ten
 I blotted for its sake.

And even more provoked
 By my officious heart
Whose emblems of desire
 From every corner start :
So little joy I find
 In their superfluous play
I curse the spell that drives
 My only love away.

THE MILLER'S MAN

THE IMPERTURBABLE miller's man
 Whose help the boy implored, drowning,
 Drifting slowly past the mill,
Was a stout swimmer, yet would not come between
The river-god and his assured victim.

Soon he too, swimming in the sun,
Is caught with cramp ; and the boy's ghost
Jeers from the reeds and rushes.
But he drowns valiantly in silence,
This being no one's business but his own.

Let us not reckon the miller's man
With Judas or with Jesus,
But with the cattle, who endure all weathers,
Or with the mill-wheel foolishly creaking,
Incurious of the grain in the bins.

JULY 24th

JULY THE TWENTY-FOURTH, a day
Heavy with clouds that would not spill
On the disconsolate earth.

Across the road in docile chorus
School-children raised their morning hymn to God
Who still forgot their names and their petitions.

'What an age to be born in!' cried old Jamboree.
'Two world wars in one generation!'
'However,' said I, 'the plum crop should be heavy!'

What was the glass doing? The glass was low.
The Germans claimed to have stormed the town of Rostov.
Sweeden dismissed the claim as premature.

Not a single painter left in the neighbourhood—
All were repainting ruined Exeter.
We had no earthly right to grumble... No?

I was reading a book about bone artifacts
In the age of the elk or woolly rhinoceros.
Already, it seems, man had a high culture.

A clerk wrote from the Ministry of Labour
To ask what reasons (if any) would prevent me
From serving in the Devonshire Home Guard.

Soon the Americans would be here : the patter
Of their rubber heels sounding like summer rain.
So pleasantly passed my forty-seventh birthday.

SAFE RECEIPT OF A CENSORED LETTER

A S THE WAR LENGTHENED, the mail shrank :
And now the Military Censor's clerk
Caught up with correspondence twelve months old—
But letters in a foreign language waited
Five months more.

'Time,' he said, 'is the best Censor :
Secret movements of troops and guns, even,
Become historical, cease to concern.
These uninterpretable items may be
Passed at last.'

Your letter was among the favoured—
Dateless familiar gossip of the village.
Thus you (who died a year ago) succeed,
Old rogue, in circumventing a more rigid
Censorship.

THE BLOTTED COPY BOOK

HE BROKE school bounds, he dared defy
The Master's atrabilious eye,
Diced, swigged raw brandy, used foul oaths,
Wore shamelessly Corinthian clothes,
And taught St. Dominic's to mock
At gown and hood and whipping-block.

The boy's a nabob now, retired
With wealth enough to be admired
Even by the School Governors
(Benignly sycophantic bores)
Who call on him to give away
Prize medals on Foundation Day

Will he at last, or will he not,
His yellowing copy-book unblot :
Accede, and seriously confess
A former want of seriousness,
Or into a wild fury burst
With : ' Let me see you in Hell first !' ?

SUMMARY

THIS BOOK was printed at the Marlborough College Press, by M. J. Freeth, J. M. Strong, R. J. B. Sweet, J. B. Wright, and P. W. Howard. The text was hand set in Monotype Walbaum and the book was printed on a Royal Wharfedale made at Otley, on Norseman Cartridge supplied by L. S. Dixon Ltd.

The printers would like to thank Mr Robert Graves for revising these poems and allowing them to be printed by the M. C. P. They would also like to thank Mr H. Andrew Freeth for his drawing of Mr Graves, and Mr E. J. Brent for his continual help and advice.

The printers' thanks are also due to the Master and other members of Common Room whose patronage has made this book possible and to all the members of the press for the various help they have given. Finally they should like to thank R. Hylton-Stewart for helping with the distribution and other jobs connected with the printing.

This edition is limited to 750 copies, 400 bound in full morocco leather and 350 in buckram cloth, of which this is

NUMBER : **122**